THE CHINESE INVENT
Papermaking

Sean Bergin

New York

Jointly published in 2021 by Sinolingua Co., Ltd., Beijing, China, and
The Rosen Publishing Group, Inc., New York, New York, United States.

Copyright © 2021 by The Rosen Publishing Group, Inc.

All rights reserved. No part of this book may be reproduced in any form without permission in writing from the publisher, except by a reviewer.

First Edition

Editor: John Kemmerer
Designer: Rachel Rising

Photo credits: Cover VW84/iStock/Getty Images; cover, pp. 1, 3, 4, 5, 7, 8, 9, 11, 12, 13, 15, 16, 17, 19, 20, 21, 23, 24, 25, 27, 28, 29, 31, 32, 33, 35, 36, 37, 39, 40, 41, 42, 43, 44, 45, 46, 47, 48 (background) Sylfida/Shutterstock.com; pp. 4, 8, 12, 16, 20, 24, 28, 32, 36, 40, 42 Valentin Agapov/Shutterstock.com; p. 5 Jacob Lund/Shutterstock.com; p. 6 tdub303/E+/Getty Images; p. 7 Melinda Podor/Moment/Getty Images; p. 9 KernelNguyen/Shutterstock.com; p. 10 dem10/E+/Getty Images; p. 13 Sun Xuejun/Shutterstock.com; p. 14 Wikimedia Commons/File:I Ching Song Dynasty print.jpg/PD; p. 17 Pictures from History/Bridgeman Images; p. 18 Jane Rix/Shutterstock.com; p 21 DragonImages/Alamy Stock Photo; p. 22 The Metropolitan Museum of Art, New York, Bequest of John M. Crawford Jr., 1988; p. 25 Sovfoto/Universal Images Group/Getty Images; p. 26 Fine Art/Corbis Historical/Getty Images; p. 29 My Portfolio/Shutterstock.com; p. 30 CPA Media Pte Ltd/Alamy Stock Photo; p.33 from Les Makamat de Hariri, courtesy Bibliothèque nationale de France; p. 34 Wikimedia Commons/File:Hydraulic-Powered Trip Hammers.jpg/PD; p. 37 © British Library Board, All Rights Reserved/Bridgeman Images; p. 38 Luisa Ricciarini/Bridgeman Images; p. 41 Peter Burger/Wikimedia Commons/File:FG Keller's original grinding machine - Museum (Germany).jpg/CC BY-SA 3.0; p. 43 Rafa Elias/Moment/Getty Images.

Some of the images in this book illustrate individuals who are models. The depictions do not imply actual situations or events.

Cataloging-in-Publication Data

Names: Bergin, Sean.
Title: The Chinese invent papermaking / Sean Bergin.
Description: New York : Rosen Publishing, 2021. | Series: Crazy cool China | Includes glossary and index.
Identifiers: ISBN 9781499469127 (pbk.) | ISBN 9781499469134 (library bound) | ISBN 9781499469141 (ebook)
Subjects: LCSH: Paper—Juvenile literature. | Papermaking—Juvenile literature. | Papermaking—China—History—Juvenile literature. | Inventions—China—History—Juvenile literature.
Classification: LCC TS1105.5 B474 2022 | DDC 676—dc23

Manufactured in the United States of America

CPSIA Compliance Information: Batch #BSRYA22. For further information contact Rosen Publishing, New York, New York, at 1-800-237-9932.

Contents

PAPERMAKING: ONE OF THE "FOUR
   GREAT INVENTIONS" OF CHINA 4
WRITING BEFORE PAPER 8
EARLY CHINESE WRITING MATERIALS 12
THE INVENTION OF PAPER....................16
PAPER AND THE SPREAD OF LITERACY 20
ONE INVENTION LEADS TO ANOTHER..........24
PAPER SPREADS TO THE ISLAMIC WORLD......28
THE BEGINNINGS OF A PAPER INDUSTRY 32
EUROPE EMBRACES PAPER....................36
THE MASS POPULARITY OF PAPER 40
CELEBRATE CHINA! 42
GLOSSARY 44
FOR MORE INFORMATION 45
BIBLIOGRAPHY 47
INDEX 48

Papermaking:
One of the "Four Great Inventions" of China

In our digital age, we take paper for granted. It's all around us, cheap and easily available, but we do not always feel it is essential to our lives. After all, we can use our smartphones and other devices to send texts and email, make notes, perform research, get the news, and read entire books. Yet, hard as it is to imagine, paper has not always been available to us, and civilization was held back without it. Once paper was invented, it became highly prized and utterly transformed the world.

For most of human history, we did not know how to make paper. Written information was carved into stone,

The Chinese discovered that paper could be made relatively quickly, easily, and cheaply, and it had many uses. In fact, the Chinese first used paper primarily as a packing, padding, and wrapping material. It wasn't until about 200 CE that it was commonly used for writing. Paper also allowed the Chinese to invent tea bags, envelopes, paper money, printing, and even toilet paper!

bone, and clay tablets. It could also be painted or inked onto sheets of leather, bamboo, wood, or silk. This made books rare, expensive to create and purchase, and very difficult to carry and transport. This also meant that, for thousands of years, very few people had access to books or learned how to read and write.

This all changed—quickly and dramatically—with the discovery of papermaking. We have the Chinese to thank for the invention of paper, beginning around the second century BCE. It was at this time that a process was gradually discovered and improved upon that used plant fibers to create a smooth, even, lightweight material we know as paper. It was made from mulberry bark, flax fibers, **hemp** waste, old rags, and even discarded fishing nets.

Even in today's digital world, paper is still all around us and something we use every day.

A man makes paper using traditional methods, separating pulp and fiber from water.

What would our daily lives be like without paper? We would have no books or magazines, for a start. There would be no paper money, only coins. We would have nothing with which to wrap our presents, box our shipments, hold our purchases from grocery and clothing stores, or contain our sketches and notes and thoughts. We would have no tissues or paper towels. And, perhaps worst of all, we would have no toilet paper!

Knowledge of papermaking spread from China to the Islamic world and then Europe beginning around the eighth century, and the world was forever changed. The majority of people learned how to read and write, and knowledge was shared far and wide. Civilizations flourished around the globe, and the lives of ordinary people were greatly enriched. By inventing paper, the Chinese gave the world one of the greatest gifts in history, gorgeously gift-wrapped!

Paper comes in all shapes, sizes, colors, and textures.

Writing Before Paper

Before the papermaking process was invented by the Chinese around the second century BCE, humans were using several different ways to record and convey information in written form. Each of the materials used to record and deliver information, however, was **inefficient**, expensive, or **cumbersome**.

The earliest examples of preserved writing are found on carved stones and bones. Wet clay was also used to preserve a civilization's

An alternative writing material known as parchment was used by ancient Egyptians, Assyrians, and Babylonians stretching back as far as the twenty-fourth century BCE. It was newly popularized by the ancient Greeks in around the fifth century BCE, possibly due to a shortage of increasingly expensive papyrus. Parchment was made from the skin of goats, sheep, and cows. The skin was scraped and then dried after being pulled and hung tightly.

history, **sacred** writings, and day-to-day record-keeping. The information was carved into the wet clay tablets with a **stylus**. The tablets were then left out in the sun to dry and harden or fired in kilns. The sun-dried tablets were **fragile** and easily broken, but they could be soaked in water, their carvings "erased." They could then be reused. The kiln-fired tablets were far more durable and permanent.

As early as the 3000s BCE, the ancient Egyptians had invented papyrus, a material similar to paper. In fact, the word "paper" is derived from "papyrus." It was made from the pith, or stem tissue, of a wetland plant called *Cyperus papyrus*. The papyrus plant grew along the Nile River delta. Thin strips of

Inscriptions of a Chinese poem were on display at the Yellow Crane Tower in Wuhan, China, in 2019.

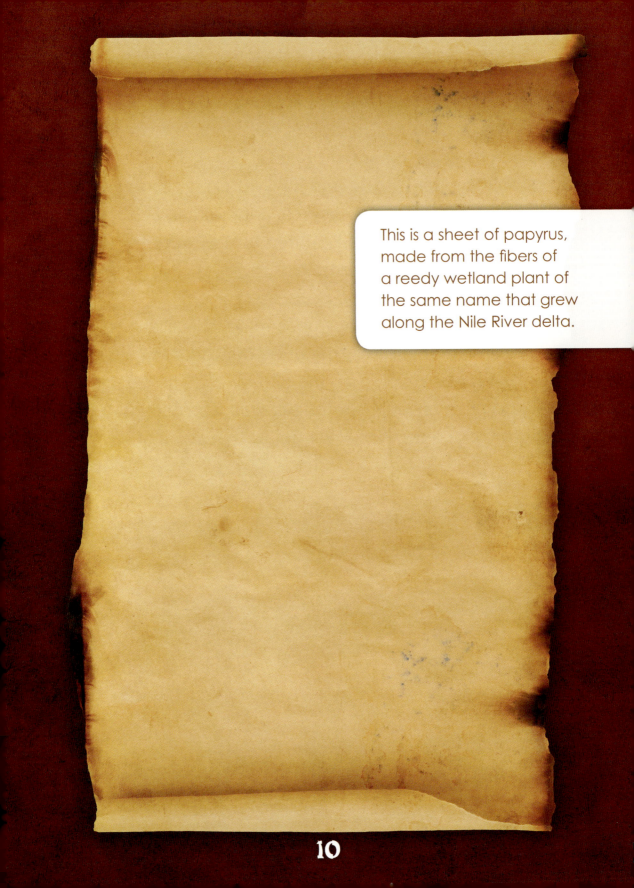

This is a sheet of papyrus, made from the fibers of a reedy wetland plant of the same name that grew along the Nile River delta.

Parchment was more durable than papyrus in both damp and dry climates, though it was more expensive and difficult to make. It was also smoother and more pliable than papyrus and could be folded into small pages that would then be bound into a book form known as a codex. Codices (the plural form of "codex") were easier to hold, carry, and store than scrolls. They were also more convenient to read, since turning pages was easier than continuously unrolling a scroll.

other, forming a sheet. A second layer of papyrus strips would be placed over the first sheet, with the second layer's strips placed at right angles to those of the first. The two sheets were then pounded together.

The result was a strong and durable piece of writing material, but one whose surface was uneven and bumpy. This made writing somewhat difficult and occasionally illegible (or difficult to read). The long sheets of papyrus were typically rolled into scrolls. When a scroll was rolled and unrolled a lot of times, the papyrus strips would eventually begin to split apart. In addition, longer texts required very large or multiple scrolls, making them hard to carry, read, store, and transport.

Early Chinese Writing Materials

Hundreds of years before they discovered how to make paper, the Chinese wrote on bone, bamboo, and even silk.

During the Shang (1600–1046 BCE) and Zhou (1046–256 BCE) dynasties, most Chinese documents were written on bone or bamboo. Text would be carved directly into animal bones, usually in the form of **pictographic** characters, and these were used to help predict the future.

The oldest surviving documents written in the Chinese language are **oracle** bones. These are usually ox shoulder blades or turtle shells into which have been carved questions to which answers would be sought through **divination**. The bone would be heated until it cracked, and the diviner would "read," or interpret, the cracks to find the answer to the question carved into the bone. Questions might be "Will it rain today?" or "Will there be misfortune this week?"

Bamboo would be cut into long, narrow strips that were about as long as one chopstick and as wide as two. Two or three dozen characters could be written in column form on a single strip. For longer texts, the strips would be collected, sewn together with leather or string, and rolled up into a kind of scroll or folded into a book shape.

Less commonly, silk was used as a writing surface. The most famous Chinese silk **manuscript** is the Chu Silk Manuscript from around 300 BCE. Its main subject matter is astrology and astronomy. The Mawangdui Silk Texts, from around 168 BCE, include the earliest known copies of the famous religious and **philosophical** writings

This is an example of a Chinese oracle bone, with pictographic characters carved into the bone.

13

This is a page from a Song era (960–1279 CE) manuscript copy of the *I Ching*. It is printed on paper, but earlier versions would have been copied on silk.

> The Chu Silk Manuscript includes material on divination, mathematics, creation myths, the origins of the universe, the structure and organization of the heavens, ancient religious beliefs and rituals, and the religious and spiritual meaning of the calendar year and the seasons. It is only about 18.5 inches (47 cm) long and 15 inches (38 cm) wide. Sometime between 1934 and 1942, it was discovered not by archaeologists but by grave robbers!

known as the *I Ching* and the *Tao Te Ching*. Also included is material on military strategy, mathematics, archery, writing, horsemanship, mapmaking, and music.

All of these writing materials had obvious drawbacks and limitations. Bone provided neither a flat nor smooth surface (though, with much labor, it could be smoothed). It also wasn't flexible, so storing it was awkward and difficult. Bone was also heavy, as was bamboo, which made reading and transporting texts written on these materials a real struggle. Silk, while very light, was far too expensive to use as an "everyday" writing material.

A writing material that was lightweight but durable, easy to write on and easy to read, able to be efficiently stored and transported, was sorely needed. And the Chinese were about to discover it!

The Invention of Paper

Credit for the invention of paper in China is usually given to a man named Cai Lun, an official in the court of the Han Dynasty. He was director of the Imperial Workshops at the Han capital of Luoyang. Cai Lun is said to have invented paper in 105 CE, but it is more likely that he developed an improved way of making paper, creating a formal "recipe" and systematizing its **manufacture**.

Cai Lun submitted his new papermaking process to Emperor He, who was so pleased with it that he gave Cai Lun an aristocratic title and made him very wealthy. However, following the death of Emperor He and his wife, a new emperor rose to power and ordered Cai Lun's arrest. Rather than report to prison, Cai Lun took a bath, dressed in his finest silk robes, and killed himself by drinking poison.

There is evidence of Chinese manufacture and use of paper dating back to around 179–141 BCE. The earliest surviving paper fragment dates to this time. It is part of a map found in Gansu Province, in northwest China. Paper fragments dating to the first century BCE have also been found elsewhere in China.

The first- and second-century-BCE paper fragments were made from hemp. One theory states that the discovery of papermaking was accidental and related to laundry! Clothes and rags made of hemp were pounded and washed in water. This left behind a hemp **residue** that could be collected and used for other purposes. At some point in the second century BCE, it was discovered that the residue could be soaked in water, pounded with a large wooden mallet, and poured into a flat mold. The remaining water dripped away or evaporated, and the result was a sheet of hemp-fiber paper!

Cai Lun, considered the inventor of paper, is shown here collecting hemp residue and separating it from water on a screen.

Over time, Cai Lun's "recipe" was improved upon. Sandalwood bark became prized for fine papermaking. Stems of grasses and vegetable matter began to be used. Rattan fibers replaced hemp fibers. Bamboo fibers, in turn, replaced rattan. The preference for fast-growing bamboo over rattan was a sign of paper's runaway success in China—the rattan plant grew too slowly to meet the Chinese demand for paper and most of it had been cut down!

The exact papermaking formula used by Cai Lun in the early second century CE is unknown, but it is thought that, in addition to hemp waste, he mixed in the bark of mulberry trees, other barks and plant fibers, shredded cloth rags, and old fishing nets. The mix was soaked in water, pressed, and placed on wooden frames or screens for drying. The end result of this process were sheets of paper that were much higher in quality than the earliest forms of hemp-fiber paper and far superior to the older alternatives of bone, bamboo, and silk.

Bamboo harvested from groves like this one helped feed the fast-growing demand for paper in China.

Paper and the Spread of Literacy

Thanks to Cai Lun, a new material had been invented that seemed perfect for the purposes of writing. His paper was smooth, lightweight, and durable. Believe it or not, however, paper in China was not used for writing, at least not at first. Paper was first used as a wrapping and packing material. It was often used to wrap and provide padding for delicate bronze mirrors when they were being moved and stored. Paper also provided a protective wrapping or envelope for poisonous substances that were sometimes used as medicine.

> Following the invention of paper, most Chinese "books" continued to be scrolls. The individual pieces of paper would be pasted together to form one long strip, which would then be wound around a wooden roller and attached to a thin wooden dowel. Books that took the form of a codex—paper cut and bound into pages between two covers—would begin appearing during the Tang Dynasty (618–907 CE).

Sometime in the third century CE, the Chinese began using paper for writing, while continuing to use it as wrapping and padding. Soon China became a world leader in book production. Scrolls and books became easier to make, carry, and store. Complete texts no longer had to be separated into several bundles, as they were when heavy and rigid bamboo strips were used. Nor did they require carts to be transported from one place to another. Instead, even longer works could be bound in one relatively lightweight volume that could be held in the hands and carried about easily. This allowed libraries to collect and store many more books and scrolls. It also created a new class of private collectors, who created their own libraries and sparked a huge demand for more and new books.

A traditional healer wraps natural medicines, such as roots and berries, in a paper packet.

By the tenth century CE, Chinese-made paper came in all sizes and colors. The finest paper was set aside for special purposes, like calligraphy, illustration, and painted scenes. Such paper was usually made of rice, sandalwood bark, hibiscus stalks, wheat straw, and even seaweed. These materials resulted in paper that had unique textures, patterns, and colors. Official government documents were dyed with a yellow substance that had the added benefit of repelling paper-destroying insects.

Knowledge and learning began to both increase and spread, benefiting a large swath of Chinese society, not just the small elite. **Literacy** increased as more and more Chinese people learned how to read and sought out books. These developments were not uniform throughout China, however. By the early fifth century, literacy and demand for books seems to have been stronger in the south, where some private libraries—the collections of individuals—could feature several thousand books. In the north at the same time, a palace library might contain only a few thousand titles.

The finest Chinese paper was reserved for calligraphy, drawings, illustrations, and paintings. This fourteenth-century drawing by the artist Ni Zan is titled "Enjoying the Wilderness in an Autumn Grove."

One Invention Leads to Another

The development of the papermaking process allowed the Chinese to introduce several other inventions that became—and remain—central to our daily lives. In the centuries following Cai Lun's innovation, the Chinese invented tea bags, paper cups and napkins, envelopes, paper money, woodblock printing, and the world's first newspaper. In the late sixth century, the Chinese gave the world something that we now use every day of our lives—toilet paper!

Before the invention of paper, the Chinese used rolls of silk, gold and silver **ingots**, and copper coins as forms of payment and exchange. But carrying silver and gold around was often dangerous, and coins were heavy. Merchants began using paper receipts that could be "cashed in" at the local treasury for a corresponding amount of ingots. Eventually, the government created a **monopoly** on these receipts and was the only one to issue "paper money."

The Chinese soon discovered that paper was very versatile and had many practical uses. In the home, paper could be used to create windows, as well as screens, curtains, walls, and sheets. People made hats out of paper, as well as umbrellas, kites, and playing cards. When stiffened, paper was even used to make armor! Beginning in the Han Dynasty (206 BCE–220 CE), the Chinese used paper to make innovative color-coded **topographical** and military maps that very accurately recorded local features.

The combination of paper with other inventions, technologies, or tools increased the reach and influence of the arts, literature, learning, and religion in Chinese society and beyond. In fact, paper would eventually be considered one of the "Four Treasures of the Scholar's Studio," along with ink, the inkstone,

Chinese papermakers place newly created wet paper sheets on a wall to dry. The man in the lower right stokes a fire to speed the drying process.

This is a page from the *Diamond Sutra*, a 16-foot (5 m) scroll made around 868 CE and the oldest surviving printed book.

The world's earliest woodblock prints are Chinese. They depict flowers and were printed on silk in three colors sometime before 220 CE. The oldest woodblock print on hemp paper dates to 650–670 CE. It is a Chinese Buddhist **mantra** meant to protect and bless the person reading or reciting it. The world's earliest printed book is a Chinese scroll known as the *Diamond Sutra*, from about 868 CE.

and the brush. The use of brush and ink on paper made painting, **calligraphy**, and poetry the highest and most respected art forms in China. The Chinese invention of block printing sometime in the eighth century CE led to the mass printing, distribution, and study of earlier Chinese literary classics and inspired much new writing. Buddhist monks, in particular, took advantage of printing and paper to mass produce prayers, charms, sutras, and sacred texts. The spread of these religious texts greatly increased Buddhism's influence within China and far beyond its borders.

Paper and printing continued to develop and evolve together. When moveable metal type was invented by the Chinese in the eleventh century, paper became thicker to be able to withstand the heavier pounding of the metal type.

Paper Spreads to the Islamic World

Chinese paper was so **innovative** and of such high quality that there was demand for it far beyond China's borders. It was soon traveling through much of the known world and being sold in foreign markets thanks to the Silk Road. This was a network of trade routes—both land and sea—that wound throughout East Asia, Southeast Asia, South Asia, Persia (Western Asia), East Africa, the Arabian Peninsula, and Southern Europe. It is named for Chinese silk, which was its most important trade good, beginning in the 200s CE during the Han Dynasty.

> The Chinese prisoners seized at the Battle of Talas were taken to the Central Asian city of Samarkand, an important Silk Road city lying between China and the Mediterranean Sea. Soon thereafter, the city developed water-powered **pulp** mills and began binding books with silk thread and leather-covered boards. Yet some historians claim that paper was known and used in Samarkand decades before the Battle of Talas.

In addition to silk, tea, spices, jade, glassware and silverware, gold, perfumes, wool, and horses were traded from region to region along these routes. Technology, too, traveled the Silk Road. Another revolutionary Chinese invention—gunpowder—was introduced to the world via the Silk Road.

While the Chinese seemed to be comfortable with their paper being sold in global markets, they did not want knowledge of the papermaking process to spread to other countries. They wanted to keep a monopoly on the knowledge and ability to make paper. The papermaking industry was based in central China, but as early as the late second century, knowledge of

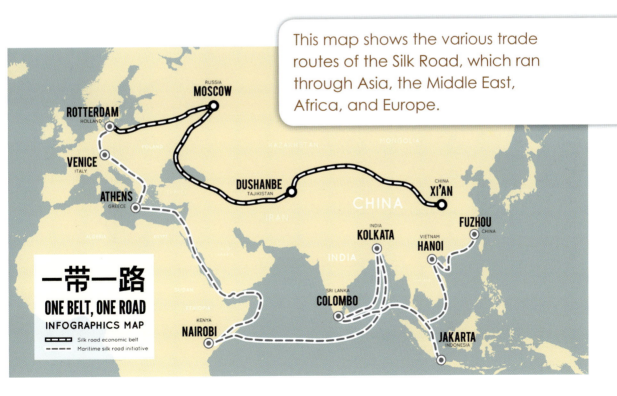

This map shows the various trade routes of the Silk Road, which ran through Asia, the Middle East, Africa, and Europe.

Workers in a Baghdad paper mill make paper using knowledge of techniques that traveled to them from China along the Silk Road.

Paper was being made in Egypt by about 900 CE, in Morocco by about 1100, and Persia by the 1200s. Baghdad and Samarkand remained famous for papermaking even after the technology spread throughout the Islamic world. Baghdad's bazaar had a special "paper market," with over 100 paper and book shops. A twelfth-century street in Marrakesh, Morocco, is named Kutubiyyin, or "Booksellers' Street," because it contained over 100 bookstores.

how to make paper was spreading to outer provinces, particularly in the northwest of China. By the seventh century CE, knowledge of papermaking had traveled to Vietnam, Korea, Japan, and India, possibly spread by Buddhist monks. China tried to shut down these competing papermaking sites but was unable to do so.

What remained of the "secret" of Chinese papermaking was lost for good in 751 CE, when the Chinese army was defeated by the forces of the Ottoman Turks at the Battle of Talas. The knowledge and skills of captured Chinese papermakers were put to use, and Baghdad and Samarkand soon became important centers of paper production. This opened up the entire Middle East, Asia Minor, and, eventually, Europe, to Chinese papermaking techniques.

The Beginnings of a Paper Industry

Having acquired the knowledge necessary to make paper, the Islamic world embraced the new material quickly and enthusiastically. As early as the eighth century CE, paper began replacing parchment in Baghdad, the capital of the Abbasid **caliphate**, for official documents. Beginning in the ninth century, important libraries throughout the Muslim world began rapidly expanding their collections. Soon, the libraries in Baghdad, Cairo, and Córdoba held more books than did those in China.

An important Muslim papermaking innovation was the substitution of linen for the bamboo, rattan, and mulberry bark used by Chinese papermakers. Because linen and rags had already been processed and bleached in the sun, there was less work to do than there would be trying to break down tree fibers and bark. Some paper recipes did, however, call for fig tree bark. Small amounts of hemp, silk, wool, cotton, and reed were also used.

Initially, making high-quality paper was a long and complicated process, requiring about twelve days per batch. Linen waste and rags went through numerous cycles of soaking, fermenting, beating, and drying through squeezing and pressing. This is the pulping stage. The resulting pulp was then formed into balls, and these were pressed into sheets. The paper was then stuck to exterior walls and allowed to dry in the sun.

Baghdad was an early center of paper manufacturing. Technology was developed there that allowed for bulk production of thick, durable paper, with far less labor. Human- or animal-powered pulp mills gave way to water-powered ones. Water-powered trip hammers also performed the pounding of the bark,

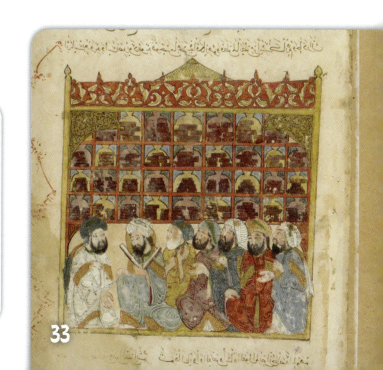

The thirteenth-century Baghdad artist Yahya ibn Mahmud al-Wasiti made this illustration of a teacher and his pupils gathered in a library. Books can be seen on the shelves behind them.

The pounding trip hammers in this drawing are powered by the waterwheel, which is set in motion by the streaming river water.

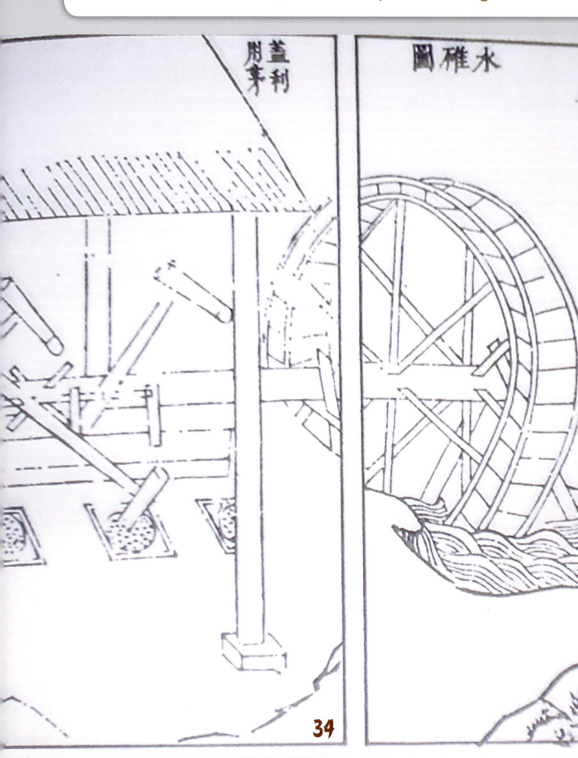

To increase the paper's strength when dry, make its surface smoother, and give it a pleasing shine, Muslim papermakers coated paper with various starches. These were derived from rice, katira (a kind of gum), white sorghum (a grain), and wheat, and sometimes boiled with white chalk. However, starches can encourage mold growth. While this was not a problem in the hot and dry climates of the Islamic world, it was in the damp regions of Europe.

linen, and rags during the pulping stage. Laborers no longer had to do this hard work with a mortar and pestle.

    The papermaking industry spread from Baghdad to Damascus, in present-day Syria. Damascus was the main supplier of paper to Europe, which did not yet possess the knowledge necessary to make paper. From Damascus, papermaking spread to Iraq and Palestine. The first paper mill in Africa operated in Egypt around 850 CE. Soon after, another one was set up in Morocco. From there, papermaking technology leapt to Europe, via Xàtiva, Spain, around 950 CE. At this time, Spain was part of the Islamic Empire.

Europe Embraces Paper

At the same time that China and the Islamic world were building papermaking industries and improving the quality of the paper they made, most of Europe was still using papyrus and parchment for their writing and record-keeping needs.

During the time of the Roman Empire (27 BCE–476 CE), Romans preferred papyrus to parchment, and Europe continued to use papyrus for as long as it remained available. Parchment was not considered of suitable quality for important scrolls. Instead, it was used only for notebooks, bound in codex form. Because it relied upon the slaughter of animals

> Parchment and the more luxurious, high-quality vellum were the dominant writing materials in Europe until the widespread introduction of paper in the later Middle Ages. Though vellum is associated with calf skin, it could be made from the hides of a variety of young animals, including horses, donkeys, deer, pigs, sheep, goats, and even camels. A parchment Bible required the skin of 250 sheep.

for their hides, parchment was more expensive. But it was also more durable, flexible, resistant to fraying and splitting, and less likely to grow mold. In the damp climates of Europe, most papyrus manuscripts lasted only a couple of decades before **disintegrating**.

In Europe, papyrus began to become more scarce. A combination of over-harvesting and market disruptions following Arab invasions of North Africa made it harder to obtain. By the middle of the ninth century CE, Egypt was producing more paper than papyrus. By the thirteenth century, papyrus making in Egypt was a distant memory. Europe was forced to embrace parchment and paper.

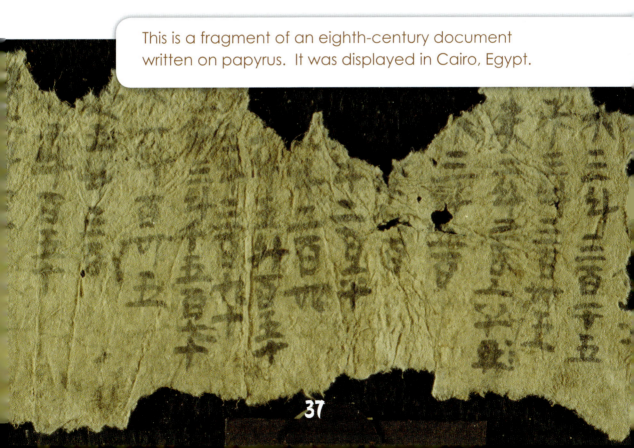

This is a fragment of an eighth-century document written on papyrus. It was displayed in Cairo, Egypt.

Workers make paper in a sixteenth-century paper workshop in Fabriano, Italy. Fabriano is where some of the world's highest quality paper was made during the medieval and Renaissance periods.

In the Americas, the Maya invented a form of papermaking—using the bark of the amate tree—as early as the first century CE. This was completely independent of and uninfluenced by the Chinese discovery of paper. The oldest surviving piece of amate is a crumpled piece of paper dating to 75 CE and was found in a tomb. The oldest known surviving book with amate pages dates from the twelfth to thirteenth century.

The Abbasid caliphate (750–1258 CE) established paper mills on the Iberian Peninsula (Spain and Portugal), in Xàtiva (1056) and Toledo (1085). This helped to create and supply a market for paper in Europe and to stoke demand. Papermaking techniques spread from the Iberian Peninsula across Europe. Between the late twelfth and early seventeenth centuries, paper mills appeared in France, Italy, Germany, Switzerland, England, Poland, Austria, the Netherlands, Denmark, and Sweden. Around 1250 CE, Arab settlers taught wool and cloth artisans in the central Italian town of Fabriano how to make high-quality paper by hand. It is believed that the quality of their work and final product—and its lower price—is what allowed paper to compete successfully against parchment and replace it as the European writing material of choice.

The Mass Popularity of Paper

European papermakers, especially those in Italy, became so efficient at making affordable quality paper that they soon came to dominate the global market. Beginning in the early fourteenth century, Europeans actually began selling paper to Arab customers. By the seventeenth century, most Arab paper mills were no longer in operation.

> Two men are credited with inventing the process for turning wood pulp into paper. In 1844, German machinist and inventor Friedrich Gottlob Keller built a wood-cut machine that extracted the fibers needed to make wood pulp, which could be used to make paper. That same year, Canadian inventor Charles Fenerty perfected a process that made paper from wood pulp, including bleaching the paper white.

The Industrial Revolution in Europe and North America brought steam-powered machines that could quickly and easily make paper with fibers from wood pulp rather than pulped rags. The resulting paper was bleached to make it white. The invention of the fountain pen and mass-produced pencils helped spur even more demand for this new industrially produced paper, which was cheap, relatively easy to make, and readily available. This, in turn, led to a boom in the availability of newspapers, schoolbooks, and books read for pleasure. Even letter writing and diary keeping became popular pastimes, thanks to a ready supply of cheap and plentiful paper. Easy access to paper allowed more and more ordinary people to learn how to read and write.

Friedrich Gottlob Keller's wood-cut machine extracted fibers from wood to create the pulp necessary to make paper.

Celebrate China!

China invented the papermaking process and spread its knowledge far and wide, transforming and benefiting the entire world. Today, China remains the largest producer of pulp and paper, with the United States just behind it in second place. Global production of pulp and paper is approaching 500 tons annually.

Increasingly, new paper is being made out of old paper—more than

Modern papermaking developments include "plastic paper." Paper is **laminated** with a layer of plastic or, in some cases, metal. This process is used to make containers, like food-takeout cups and cartons, as well as paper plates and plastic-lined paper bags. The coated paper is water resistant, difficult to tear, and seals in heat. Laminated paper products are not easy to reuse, however. In order to be recycled, the plastic layer must first be separated from the paper.

a third of the fiber used to make new paper products comes from recycled sources. Much of the world's paper recycling takes place in China, and it goes into the making of our cardboard boxes, shopping bags, notebook paper, envelopes, cartons, newspapers, and magazines!

Despite the rise of the digital era, paper sales and use continue to boom. In the US alone, the paper we use in every five-year period can cover the entire surface of the country. Thanks to China, paper is here to stay—and it is getting greener every day!

Used cardboard is piled up and ready to be recycled into new high-quality paper products, such as notebook paper, envelopes, newspapers, and magazines.

Glossary

caliphate A government, empire, or land ruled by a spiritual leader of Islam.
calligraphy Artistic and elegant handwriting.
cumbersome Hard to carry, hold, or use because of size or weight.
disintegrate To fall apart or break into pieces; to decompose.
divination The practice of trying to tell fortunes, predict future events, or discover hidden knowledge.
fragile Easily broken or destroyed; delicate.
hemp A tall Asian herb often grown for its tough fibers.
inefficient Wasteful of time or energy.
ingot A piece of metal cast into a shape that makes carrying and storing it easy and convenient.
innovative Introducing a new idea, method, or device.
laminate To bond layers of paper, wood, or fabric with resin and compress them together with heat.
literacy The ability to read and write.
mantra A spiritual prayer, spell, or incantation that is recited and repeated.
manufacture The process of making something by hand or by machine.
manuscript A written or typed document that is not mechanically printed.
monopoly Exclusive possession or control; when only one person or company owns and controls something.
oracle An answer or a decision delivered by God or a god through a human being, such as a priest or priestess.
philosophical Relating to the study of logic, ethics, and the nature of reality; relating to the search for understanding of values and reality.
pictographic Describing a system of symbols that convey meaning; involving visual language that relies on pictures instead of words.
pulp A soft mass of vegetable matter, such as plant fibers, that remains after most of its water has been squeezed out under pressure.
residue What remains after a part of a whole has been taken away or separated out.
sacred Holy; dedicated to God or a god or to the service of the divine; worthy of respect and reverence.
stylus An instrument used to write or carve into wax or clay tablets.
sutra A teaching from the Buddha; sutras form the basic texts of Buddhist scripture and sacred writings.
topographical Using detailed and accurate representation on maps or charts of natural and human-made features of a particular place or region; relating to the artistic representation of a locality.

For More Information

Asia Society (three locations)
725 Park Avenue
New York, NY 10021
(212) 288-6400

1370 Southmore Boulevard
Houston, TX 77004

9 Justice Drive
Admiralty Hong Kong
852-2103-9511

Website: https://asiasociety.org
Asia Society is the leading educational organization dedicated to promoting mutual understanding and strengthening partnerships among people, leaders, and institutions of Asia and the United States in a global context.

Chinese Historical Society of America
965 Clay Street
San Francisco, CA 94108
(415) 391-1188, ext. 101
Website: https://chsa.org
The Chinese Historical Society of America Museum is the oldest organization in the country dedicated to the interpretation, promotion, and preservation of the social, cultural, and political history and contributions of the Chinese in America.

Museum of Chinese in America
215 Centre Street
New York, NY 10013
(855) 955-MOCA
Website: http://www.mocanyc.org

Founded in 1980, the Museum of Chinese in America (MOCA) is dedicated to preserving and presenting the history, heritage, culture, and diverse experiences of people of Chinese descent in the United States.

Museum of Science and Industry, Chicago
5700 South Lake Shore
Chicago, IL 60637
(773) 684-1414
Website: https://www.msichicago.org

The Museum of Science and Industry, Chicago—one of the largest science museums in the world—is home to more than 400,000 square feet of hands-on exhibits designed to spark scientific inquiry and creativity.

National Museum of China (NMC)
No. 16 East Chang'an Street
Dongcheng District
Beijing, China 100006
Website: http://en.chnmuseum.cn
The NMC is a palace of history and art reflecting and displaying China's traditional and modern culture. It houses more than 1.4 million objects that typify and bear witness to the richness and depth of China's 5,000-year-old civilization.

Robert C. Williams Museum of Papermaking
Renewable Bioproducts Institute
Mail code 0620, Georgia Tech
Atlanta, GA 30332-0620
(404) 894-5700
Website: https://paper.gatech.edu/robert-c-williams-museum-papermaking

The Robert C. Williams Museum of Papermaking is an internationally renowned resource on the history of paper and paper technology. In addition to more than 2,000 books, the museum features a collection of over 10,000 watermarks, papers, tools, machines, and manuscripts. The museum's mission is to collect, preserve, increase, and disseminate knowledge about papermaking—past, present and future.

Bardoe, Cheryl, and the Field Museum. *China: A History*. New York, NY: Harry N. Abrams, 2019.

Basbanes, Nicholas A. *On Paper: The Everything of Its Two-Thousand-Year History*. New York, NY: Random House, 2013.

Cotterell, Arthur. *Ancient China*. New York, NY: DK Eyewitness, 2005.

Culp, Jennifer. *Ancient Chinese Technology*. New York, NY: Rosen Publishing, 2016.

Frankopan, Peter. *The Silk Roads: A New History of the World*. New York, NY: Bloomsbury Publishing, 2015.

Hanson-Harding, Brian. *Ancient Chinese Religion and Beliefs*. New York, NY: Rosen Publishing, 2016.

Harrison-Hall, Jessica. *China: A History in Objects*. London, UK: Thames & Hudson, 2018.

Hunter, Dard. *Papermaking: The History and Technique of an Ancient Craft*. Mineola, NY: Dover Publications, 2011.

Hurt, Avery Elizabeth. *Ancient Chinese Government and Geography*. New York, NY: Rosen Publishing, 2016.

Kurlansky, Mark. *Paper: Paging Through History*. New York, NY: W. W. Norton & Co., 2017.

Liu, Jing. *Barbarians and the Birth of Chinese Identity: The Five Dynasties and Ten Kingdoms to the Yuan Dynasty (907–1368)* (Understanding China Through Comics). Berkeley, CA: Stone Bridge Press, 2017.

Liu, Jing. *Division to Unification in Imperial China: The Three Kingdoms to the Tang Dynasty (220–907)* (Understanding China Through Comics). Berkeley, CA: Stone Bridge Press, 2016.

Liu, Jing. *Foundations of Chinese Civilization: The Yellow Emperor to the Han Dynasty (2697 BCE–220 CE)* (Understanding China Through Comics). Berkeley, CA: Stone Bridge Press, 2016.

Liu, Jing. *The Making of Modern China: The Ming Dynasty to the Qing Dynasty (1368–1912)* (Understanding China Through Comics). Berkeley, CA: Stone Bridge Press, 2017.

Lusted, Marcia Amidon. *Ancient Chinese Daily Life*. New York, NY: Rosen Publishing, 2016.

Morrow, Paula. *Ancient Chinese Culture*. New York, NY: Rosen Publishing, 2016.

Wasserstrom, Jeffrey N., ed. *The Oxford Illustrated History of Modern China*. New York, NY: Oxford University Press, 2018.

Bibliography

Basbanes, Nicholas A. *On Paper: The Everything of Its Two-Thousand-Year History.* New York, NY: Random House, 2013.

Beckwith, Christopher I. *Empires of the Silk Road: A History of Central Eurasia from the Bronze Age to the Present.* Princeton, NJ: Princeton University Press, 2009.

Bloom, Jonathan M. "Papermaking: The Historical Diffusion of an Ancient Technique." Springer Link. 2017. https://link.springer.com/chapter/10.1007/978-3-319-44654-7_3.

Cartwright, Mark. "Paper in Ancient China." Ancient History Encyclopedia. 2017. https://www.ancient.eu/article/1120/paper-in-ancient-china/.

Frankopan, Peter. *The Silk Roads: A New History of the World.* New York, NY: Bloomsbury Publishing, 2015.

Harford, Tim. "How the Invention of Paper Changed the World." BBC News. 2017. https://www.bbc.com/news/the-reporters-38892687.

Hunter, Dard. *Papermaking: The History and Technique of an Ancient Craft.* Mineola, NY: Dover Publications, 2011.

Kurlansky, Mark. *Paper: Paging Through History.* New York, NY: W. W. Norton & Co., 2017.

LinchpinSEO. "Trends That Will Transform the Pulp and Paper Industry Outlook in 2020." 2019. https://linchpinseo.com/trends-pulp-and-paper-industry/.

Mote, Frederick W. *Imperial China: 900–1800.* Cambridge, MA: Harvard University Press, 1999.

Pitts, Mark. "Paper Industry Innovation: More Than You Might Think." American Forest and Paper Association. 2017. https://www.afandpa.org/media/blog/bloga/2017/10/20/paper-industry-innovation---more-than-you-might-think.

Research and Markets/Intrado Global Newswire. "China Paper and Paperboard Import Report 2019–2023." 2019. https://www.globenewswire.com/news-release/2019/04/01/1790975/0/en/China-Paper-and-Paperboard-Import-Report-2019-2023.html.

Ropp, Paul S. *China in World History.* New York, NY: Oxford University Press, 2010.

Szczepanski, Kallie. "The Invention of Paper." ThoughtCo. 2019. https://www.thoughtco.com/invention-of-paper-195265.

Wendorf, Marcia. "The Long and Complex History of Paper." Interesting Engineering. 2019. https://interestingengineering.com/the-long-and-complex-history-of-paper.

Wu, K. T. "The Chinese Book: Its Evolution and Development." China Heritage Quarterly. 2009. http://www.chinaheritagequarterly.org/tien-hsia.php?searchterm=020_chinese_book.inc&issue=020.

Zhuang, Zhong, et al. "China's Pulp and Paper Industry: A Review." Georgia Institute of Technology. Undated. Retrieved March 2020. https://cpbis.gatech.edu/files/papers/CPBIS-FR-08-03%20Zhuang_Ding_Li%20FinalReport-China_Pulp_and_Paper_Industry.pdf.

Index

A
Abbasid caliphate, 32, 39

B
Baghdad, 31, 32, 33, 35
bamboo, 5, 12, 13, 15, 19, 21, 32
bleaching of paper, 32, 40, 41
bone, 5, 8, 12, 15, 19
books, 4, 5, 7, 11, 13, 20, 21, 23, 27, 28, 31, 32, 39, 41
Buddhism/Buddhist texts, 27, 31

C
Cai Lun, 16, 19, 20, 24
calligraphy, 23, 27
Chu Silk Manuscript, 13, 15
clay tablets, 5, 8–9
codices, 11, 20, 36
currency exchange/as payment, 24

D
Damascus, 35
Diamond Sutra, 27
divination, 12, 15

E
Egypt, 8, 9, 31, 35, 37
envelopes, 4, 20, 24, 43
Europe, 7, 28, 31, 35, 36–39, 40

F
Fenerty, Charles, 40
"Four Treasures of the Scholar's Studio," 25–27

G
gunpowder, 29

H
Han Dynasty, 16, 25, 28
He, Emperor, 16
hemp, 5, 17, 19, 27, 32

I
illustration/painting, 23, 27
Industrial Revolution, 40
Iraq, 35
Islamic world, 7, 28–31, 32, 35, 36

K
Keller, Friedrich Gottlob, 40

L
libraries, 21, 23, 32
linen, 32, 33, 35
literacy/ability to read and write, 5, 7, 23, 41

M
magazines, 7, 43
maps, 25
Mawangdui Silk Texts, 13
Maya, 39
Morocco, 31, 35
moveable metal type, 27
mulberry bark, 5, 19, 32

N
newspapers, 24, 41, 43

O
oracle bones, 12

P
Palestine, 35
paper mills, 35, 39, 40
paper money, 4, 7, 24
papyrus, 8, 9–11, 36, 37
parchment, 8, 11, 32, 36–37, 39
"plastic paper," 42
pulp/pulp mills, 28, 33, 35, 40, 42

R
rattan, 19, 32
recycling/recycled paper, 42–43
Roman Empire, 36

S
sandalwood bark, 19, 23
scrolls, 11, 13, 20, 21, 27, 36
Shang Dynasty, 12
silk, 5, 12, 13, 15, 19, 24, 27, 28, 29, 32
Silk Road, 28–29
stone carving, 4, 8

T
Talas, Battle of, 28, 31
Tang Dynasty, 20
tea bags, 4, 24
toilet paper, 4, 7, 24

V
vellum, 36

W
woodblock printing, 24, 27
wood pulp, 40

Z
Zhou Dynasty, 12